write me a Poem

POKING FUN IN A POEM

by VALERIE BODDEN

Illustrations by ETIENNE DELESSERT

CREATIVE EDUCATION ▪ CREATIVE PAPERBACKS

Published by Creative Education and Creative Paperbacks
P.O. Box 227, Mankato, Minnesota 56002
Creative Education and Creative Paperbacks are imprints of The Creative Company
www.thecreativecompany.us

Design and production by Chelsey Luther
Art direction by Rita Marshall
Printed in the United States of America

Photographs by DeviantArt (Esiri76), Getty Images (Hulton Archive/stringer).
Illustrations © by Etienne Delessert. Excerpt from "This Is Just to Say," by William
Carlos Williams, from *The Collected Poems: Volume 1, 1909–1939*, © 1938 by New Directions
Publishing Corp. Reprinted by permission of New Directions Publishing Corp.

Library of Congress Cataloging-in-Publication Data
Bodden, Valerie.
Poking fun in a poem / Valerie Bodden.
p. cm. — (Write me a poem)
Includes index.
Summary: An elementary exploration of word play and attitude in poetry, introducing
puns, stanzas, and limericks as well as poets such as Edward Lear. Includes a writing
exercise.
ISBN 978-1-60818-622-8 (hardcover)
ISBN 978-1-62832-254-5 (pbk)
ISBN 978-1-56660-682-0 (eBook)
1. Poetry—Juvenile literature. 2. Puns and punning—Juvenile literature. 3. Plays on
words—Juvenile literature. 4. Humor in literature. 5. Poetry—Authorship—Juvenile
literature. I. Title.

PN1059.P86B63 2015
808.1—dc23   2015007214

CCSS: RI.1.1, 2, 3, 5, 6, 7; RI.2.1, 2, 3, 5, 6, 7; RI.3.1, 3, 5, 7; RF.1.1; RF.2.3, 4; RF.3.3

First Edition HC 9 8 7 6 5 4 3 2 1
First Edition PBK 9 8 7 6 5 4 3 2 1

Table of Contents

Knock,
Knock!

Word Play

Who's there? Boo. Boo who? Don't cry; it's only a joke! Every time you tell a knock-knock joke like this, you're playing with words. Most knock-knock jokes are funny because they use puns. Puns are jokes made from words that sound alike but have different meanings.

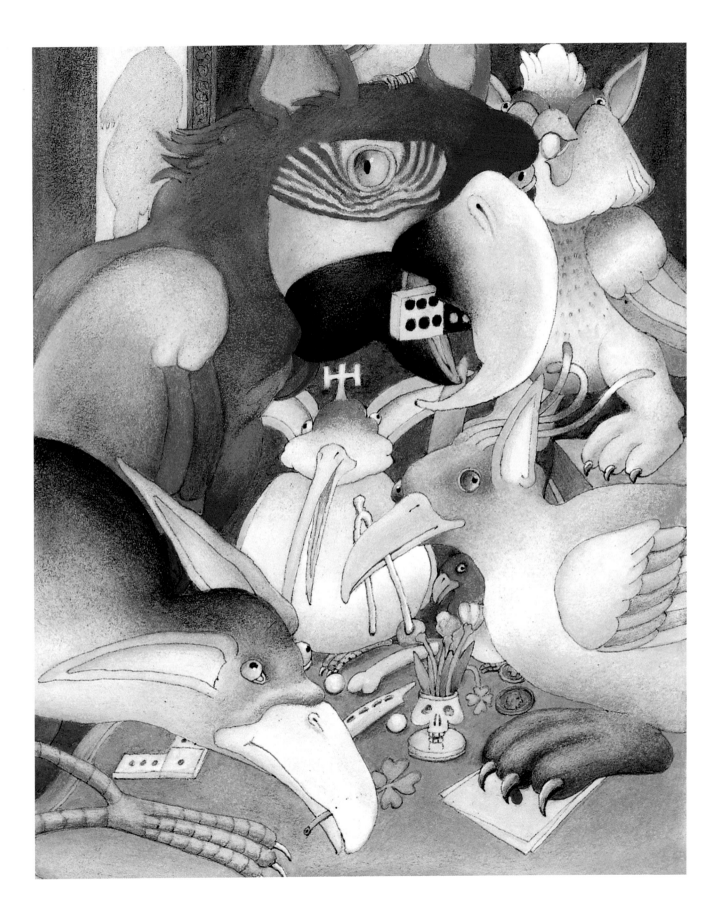

POETS love to play with words. Sometimes they use puns or make up their own **nonsense** words. Poets pick special words to help readers understand how they feel.

Puns and Readers

Puns can make readers laugh. Or they might make them take a closer look at something. In Ogden Nash's poem "A Flea and a Fly in a Flue," the poet puns on the words "fly" and "flea/flee."

A "flue" is a tube, like in a chimney.

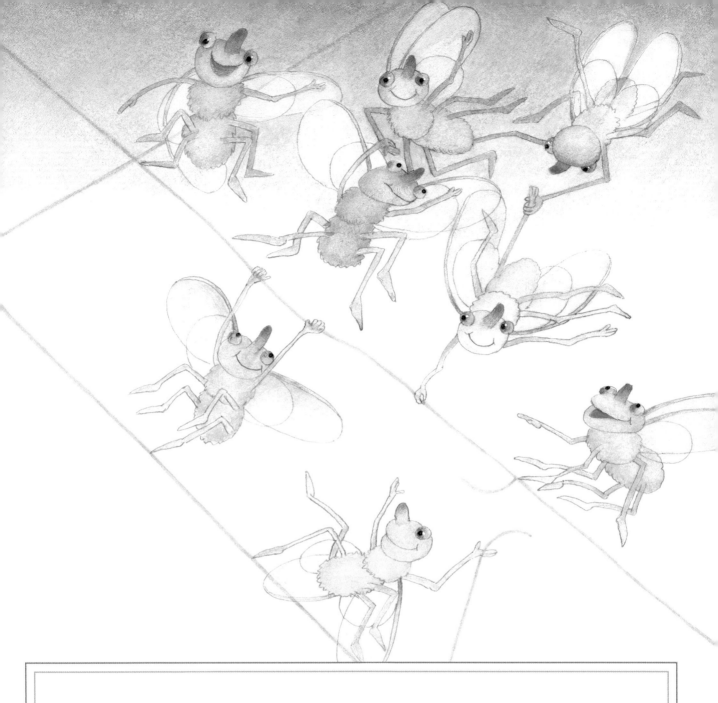

A flea and a fly in a flue
Were imprisoned, so what could they do?
Said the fly, "let us flee!"
"Let us fly!" said the flea.

Making Nonsense

Poets who write nonsense poems might make up words. Or they might put words together in funny ways that don't make sense. What doesn't make sense in the following **stanza** from "Antigonish" by Hughes Mearns?

Yesterday, upon the stair,
I met a man who wasn't there.
He wasn't there again today,
I wish, I wish he'd go away.

Dropping Hints

POKING FUN IN A POEM

Poets use **allusions** to leave hints about a familiar person, place, or thing. But they do not talk directly about those things. Can you find an allusion to a common fairy tale in these lines from Pat Mora's poem "Same Song"?

my twelve-year-old daughter

...

outlines her mouth in Neon Pink

peers into the mirror, mirror on the wall

Who says the famous line, "Mirror, mirror on the wall"?

Choosing Words

Poets choose words carefully to show their **attitude**. Some poems are playful. Others are scary or sad. In the poem "This Is Just to Say" by William Carlos Williams, do you think the speaker is really sorry? Or is he being funny?

I have eaten
the plums
that were in
the icebox
…
Forgive me
they were delicious
so sweet
and so cold

How you feel about something affects your attitude.

Poking Fun in Poems

Many different kinds of poems play with words. Limericks are funny, five-line poems that often use puns. Other poems use serious puns to make readers think. In William Shakespeare's *Romeo and Juliet*, Romeo refuses to dance. He puns on the words "soles" (the bottom of a shoe) and "soul" (feelings or spirit).

Not I, believe me. You have dancing shoes
With nimble soles; I have a soul of lead

Does a "soul of lead" sound heavy or light?

Next time you read a poem, pay attention to how the poet plays with words. It might make you want to cry or laugh out loud!

Famous Poet: Edward Lear

ENGLISH

poet Edward Lear was born in 1812. He became well known for his limericks. Most were nonsense poems, like "There Was an Old Man with a Beard."

There was an Old Man with a beard,
Who said, "It is just as I feared!—
Two Owls and a Hen,
Four Larks and a Wren,
Have all built their nests in my beard!"

The first and last lines of Edward's limericks often ended in the same word.

Activity:
Write Me a Poem

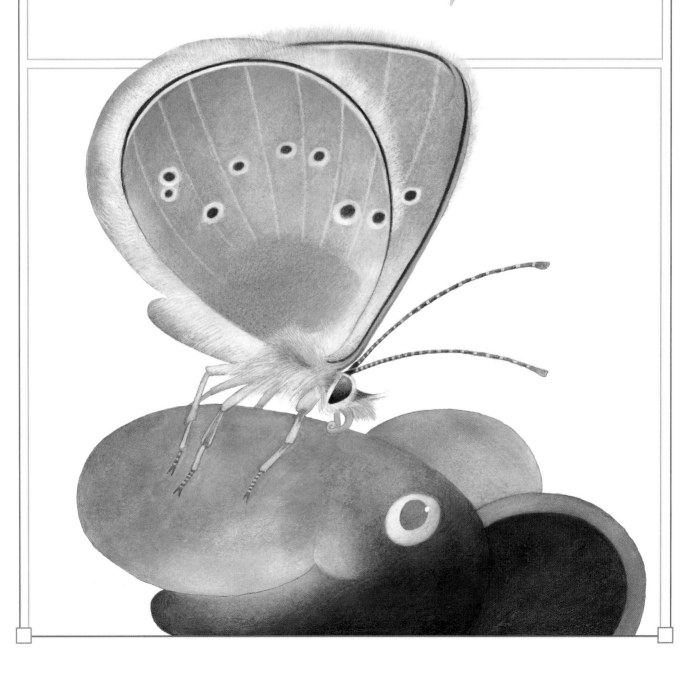

MAKE a list of your favorite words.

Try to put parts of two of the words together to make a new word. (For example, "turtle" and "purple" could become "turple" or "purtle.") Now write a nonsense poem using your new word. Remember, the words in a nonsense poem don't have to make sense!

Putting red and yellow together makes a color—and a nonsense word!

21

Glossary

allusions	things that are hinted at but not talked about directly
attitude	how a writer feels about his or her subject
nimble	quick and easy to move
nonsense	words that are silly or have no meaning
stanza	a group of lines that make up part of a poem

Read More

Corbett, Pie. *Poem-maker, Word-shaker*. North Mankato, Minn.: Chrysalis, 2006.

Magee, Wes. *How to Write Poems*. Laguna Hills, Calif.: QEB, 2007.

Prelutsky, Jack. *Read a Rhyme, Write a Rhyme*. New York: Knopf, 2005.

Websites

Poetry 4 Kids: How to Write Funny Poetry
http://www.poetry4kids.com/modules.php?name=Content&pa=showpage&pid=5
Poet Kenn Nesbitt teaches kids how to write puns.

Scholastic: Writing with Writers
http://teacher.scholastic.com/Writewit/poetry/
Listen to poets read some of their poems and check out their tips for writing poetry.

Index